This motivational journal belongs to:

Published 2024
Printed in the United States of America

First Edition
ISBN (softcover): 978-1-963380-09-5
ISBN (hardcover): 978-1-963380-10-1

For information, address:
Holzer Books LLC
8 The Green, Ste. A
Dover, Delaware 19901 USA

For information about special discounts available for bulk purchases, sales promotions, and educational needs, contact:
info@holzerbooksllc.com
+1 (888) 901-7776

# CREED OF A TEAM

by BENNY SERNA

We take calculated risks.

We live and think outside the box.

We are the example.

We trust our instincts.

We believe in each other.

We state the facts free from our personal opinions.

We never compromise our integrity.

We exceed expectations.

We envision our goals daily.

We are not afraid of making decisions.

We don't look back.

We speak with purpose.

We are committed.

We never give up.

***We are One.***

*We take calculated risks.*

*We live and think outside the box.*

*We are the example.*

*We trust our instincts.*

*We believe in each other.*

*We state the facts free from our personal opinions.*

*We never compromise our integrity.*

*We exceed expectations.*

*We envision our goals daily.*

*We are not afraid of making decisions.*

*We don't look back.*

*We speak with purpose.*

*We are committed.*

*We are one.*

*We take calculated risks.*

*We live and think outside the box.*

*We are the example.*

*We trust our instincts.*

*We believe in each other.*

*We state the facts free from our personal opinions.*

*We never compromise our integrity.*

*We envision our goals daily.*

*We are not afraid of making decisions.*

*We don't look back.*

*We speak with purpose.*

*We are committed.*

*We are one.*

*We take calculated risks.*

*We live and think outside the box.*

*We trust our instincts.*

*We believe in each other.*

*We state the facts free from our personal opinions.*

*We never compromise our integrity.*

*We exceed expectations.*

*We are not afraid of making decisions.*

*We don't look back.*

*We speak with purpose.*

*We never give up.*

*We are one.*

*We take calculated risks.*

*We live and think outside the box.*

*We are the example.*

*We trust our instincts.*

*We believe in each other.*

*We state the facts free from our personal opinions.*

*We never compromise our integrity.*

*We exceed expectations.*

*We envision our goals daily.*

*We are not afraid of making decisions.*

*We don't look back.*

*We speak with purpose.*

*We never give up.*

*We are one.*

*We take calculated risks.*

*We live and think outside the box.*

*We trust our instincts.*

*We believe in each other.*

*We state the facts free from our personal opinions.*

*We never compromise our integrity.*

*We exceed expectations.*

*We envision our goals daily.*

*We are not afraid of making decisions.*

*We don't look back.*

*We speak with purpose.*

*We are committed.*

*We never give up.*

*We are one.*

*We take calculated risks.*

*We live and think outside the box.*

*We are the example.*

*We trust our instincts.*

*We believe in each other.*

*We state the facts free from our personal opinions.*

*We never compromise our integrity.*

*We envision our goals daily.*

*We don't look back.*

*We speak with purpose.*

*We are committed.*

*We are one.*

*We take calculated risks.*

*We live and think outside the box.*

*We are the example.*

*We trust our instincts.*

*We believe in each other.*

*We state the facts free from our personal opinions.*

*We never compromise our integrity.*

*We exceed expectations.*

*We envision our goals daily.*

*We are not afraid of making decisions.*

*We don't look back.*

*We speak with purpose.*

*We are committed.*

*We never give up.*

*We are one.*

*We take calculated risks.*

*We are the example.*

*We trust our instincts.*

*We believe in each other.*

*We never compromise our integrity.*

*We exceed expectations.*

*We envision our goals daily.*

*We are not afraid of making decisions.*

*We don't look back.*

*We speak with purpose.*

*We are committed.*

Made in United States
Troutdale, OR
11/03/2026

56845386R00070